A PALM TREE'S CHRISTMAS WISH

By Pina Bird

Illustrated by
Jennifer Kirkham

Text and illustrations copyright © 2023 by Pina Basone, Pseudonym Pina Bird
Published by Pina Bird Books LLC

All rights reserved.

No part of this publication may be reproduced, distributed, or transmitted in any form or by any means, including photocopying, recording, or other electronic or mechanical methods, without the prior written permission of the publisher, except in the case of brief quotations embodied in reviews and certain other non-commercial uses permitted by copyright law.

A Palm Tree's Christmas Wish is a work of fiction. Names, characters, places, and incidents are the products of the author's imagination or are used fictitiously. Any resemblance to actual events, locales, or person, living or dead, is entirely coincidental.

The moral rights of the author and illustrator have been asserted.

Hardback   ISBN-978-1-7347321-6-0
Paperback   ISBN-978-1-7347321-7-7
E-book   ISBN-978-1-7347321-8-4

Library of Congress control number: 2023914349

On a cold winter's day, in a small New England town, the annual delivery of Christmas trees from Vermont Tree Farm arrived at Graham's Nursery. The air was filled with the sweet aroma of freshly cut trees as the truck doors opened. While counting the trees, a worker discovered something unusual inside.

"Holy jingle bells," the worker shouted. "Mr. Graham, come quick! Look what we have here!"

Mr. Graham hurried over but stopped suddenly when he saw one of the trees hidden in the far back of the truck. What made the tree stand out wasn't that it was too short, too tall, too wide, or too thin. What set this tree apart from the rest was that it wasn't a Christmas tree at all!

It was a palm tree! "How on Earth did this get here?" exclaimed Mr. Graham. "It seems like a silly mix-up" he cheerfully added. "Let's unload the truck and sort it out later."

After a long day of setting up Christmas trees, Mr. Graham and his staff closed the gift shop. With a yawn, he turned to his furry companion, Mr. Buttons the cat, and said, "It's time to head home!" Mr. Buttons responded with a soft meow.

Snowflakes began to dance gently from the sky and a soft hush filled the once still air. If you listened very carefully, you could hear tiny voices coming from the Christmas tree stands, as the branches playfully twirled around.

"What kind of Christmas tree is she?" whispered Birch the Fraser fir. Aspen, the Colorado blue spruce, replied with a smirk, "She's not a Christmas tree, she's a palm tree!"

"Why does it matter what kind of tree she is?" asked Ash the Douglas fir with a curious tilt of his branches. "Everyone knows what a Christmas tree looks like...and she's not it," grumbled Aspen. "She's different from us! She doesn't *belong*!"

The palm tree stood silently. Pitch the Balsam fir, admired by all the Christmas trees for his beauty and fullness, leaned closer to read the palm tree's name tag. "Phoenix! Ahh... I believe Phoenix will be a wonderful Christmas tree!" he declared. Then, bending towards Phoenix, he whispered, "Don't worry, Aspen's bark is louder than her bite."

Phoenix smiled nervously at Pitch. All she'd ever wanted was to be a Christmas tree, just like the other trees. Phoenix couldn't help but feel that her chances were quite slim with all the fuss about her not being a real Christmas tree.

As the villagers came to Graham's Nursery, searching for the perfect Christmas tree, they strolled right past Phoenix, laughing and shaking their heads as if to question, "What is she doing here?"

Phoenix could hear Aspen taunting, "You're too top-heavy."
"Eww! You smell like a coconut."

Phoenix felt disheartened, believing she would never become a Christmas tree for anyone. "Just wait," whispered Pitch gently. "Happy days lie ahead! You'll see." Phoenix lowered her head in silence.

The following day, just two days before Christmas, a family visited the nursery. A little girl pointed excitedly at Aspen, but as she approached the tree, she felt a prick from Aspen's spiny needles.

The little girl let out a yelp, and her mother rushed over to grab her tiny hand. Her father, shaking his head, decided to choose Pitch instead.

As Pitch rolled away, he felt happy but also sad to say farewell to his friend. A little tear trickled down Phoenix's trunk when she saw the SUV drive off into the distance.

Soon, Birch was swept away, followed by Ash. Only Phoenix and Aspen remained.

It wasn't long before Aspen started pestering Phoenix once again. Suddenly, they heard Mr. Graham's voice, and the trees fell silent.
"Oh no!" Mr. Graham bellowed to one of his staff members.
"We've run out of firewood and the next shipment won't arrive until after Christmas. We'll need to use one of these trees instead."
Aspen's eyes widened in fear.

Mr. Graham reached for Aspen. "Ouch!" he cried out, quickly pulling back his hand.

Phoenix realized that she needed to act fast, so she jumped in front of Aspen to protect her.

Just then a worker shouted, "Mr. Graham, Vermont Tree Farm called. They're sending a special firewood delivery today to make up for the palm tree mix-up!"

"Great news!" shouted Mr. Graham, as he happily returned to the gift shop.

"Why did you do that?" asked Aspen. "Why did you help me when I haven't been nice to you?"

Phoenix looked up nervously. "Because it was the right thing to do," she said. "It's important to treat others how you want to be treated." Then, with a playful smile, she added "by the way... I like smelling like a coconut!"

The two trees glanced at each other and burst into laughter.

"You know, Aspen," Phoenix said gently, "if you were a bit nicer, you might have found a home by now. Aspen stared at the ground. "I guess you're right... I never saw it that way. I'll try to be better from now on!"

Later in the day, a cheerful couple came by looking for the perfect tree. Aspen remembered Phoenix's words and closed her eyes. She stood straight and tall as the couple admired her. "We'll take this one!" they announced to Mr. Graham.

Phoenix gave Aspen a playful wink as she was carried away. She felt happy for Aspen but at the same time, disappointed that nobody had picked her. More than anything, Phoenix wished to be a Christmas tree. But there she was, all alone on Christmas Eve.

Late in the evening, as the clouds cleared above the nursery, the clock in the gift shop chimed midnight. The stars twinkled, and the moon cast its gentle glow upon little Phoenix.

Suddenly, as if by magic, Phoenix heard the gentle jingle of bells. She glanced up at the shimmering moon and saw something surprising.

There, riding in his sleigh, was Santa! "Whoa!" he called to his reindeer. As they gently landed, Santa hopped off and headed towards Phoenix.

"Hello Phoenix!" said Santa. Phoenix gazed at the ground and whispered shyly, "You know my name?" "Yes!" Santa responded, "I know the names of all the Christmas trees."

Phoenix sighed. "I'm not a Christmas tree. I know that now," she said sadly.

"Nonsense!" Santa uttered. "Phoenix, you have a warm heart. You stood up for Aspen even when she wasn't nice to you. That, my dear, is the true spirit we seek in a Christmas tree. To celebrate your wonderful deed, I'd be honored to adorn you with festive decorations, so that all may see the radiant light that shines brightly within you!"

Phoenix was amazed. "Could it be true? Santa wants to decorate me for Christmas?" she wondered. She nodded her head, wiped away her tears, and watched Santa adorn her with beautiful garlands, twinkling lights, and shiny ornaments.

Santa stepped back and declared, "You are the most beautiful Christmas tree I have ever seen!" With a warm smile he added, "Things are about to get even more magical!"

On Christmas morning, Phoenix awoke and was astonished to find herself surrounded by friendly villagers who had gathered to celebrate with her. They joyfully sang Christmas carols while Mr. Graham graciously offered everyone steaming mugs of rich hot cocoa and his delicious gingerbread cookies.

Phoenix stood tall, beaming with pride. Her dream to become a cherished Christmas tree had come true!

And all it took was a simple act of kindness...and a touch of Christmas magic!

THE END

TEN SIMPLE ACTS OF KINDNESS:

1. Be kind to your classmates and teachers.
2. Include others who may feel left out during playtime or school activities.
3. Share and take turns with your friends.
4. When you're introduced to someone, make eye contact, smile, and offer a handshake.
5. Always remember to say "please" and "thank you."
6. Be kind to animals.
7. Write a thank you note to express gratitude to your teacher, family member, or a classmate to brighten their day.
8. Use kind words and compliment others.
9. Volunteer in the community to help those in need.
10. Stand up for a classmate who is being bullied or treated unkindly.

Did you know that kindness contributes to a longer and healthier life? It reduces stress and brings joy to your heart. Start with one act of kindness a day, and soon it will come naturally! Embrace kindness, and happiness will surely follow!

Be kind and follow your dreams... they lead the way.

Pina Bird

Mr. Graham's Gingerbread Cookies

TOOLS YOU'LL NEED:

- Rolling Pin
- Hand Mixer
- Parchment Paper
- Baking Sheet
- Wire Cooling Rack
- Gingerbread Man Cookie Cutter

INGREDIENTS:

- 3 cups all-purpose organic flour
- 3/4 cup packed organic dark brown sugar
- 3/4 teaspoon organic baking soda
- 1 tablespoon organic ground cinnamon
- 1 tablespoon organic ground ginger
- 1/2 teaspoon organic ground cloves
- 1/2 teaspoon sea salt
- 12 tablespoons room temperature organic butter, soften
- 3/4 cup dark molasses unsulphered
- 2 tablespoons organic milk

Mr. Graham prefers using organic products. For a gluten-free option, replace traditional flour with King Arthur's 1:1 gluten-free blend.

INSTRUCTIONS:

1. In a mixing bowl, combine flour, brown sugar, baking soda, cinnamon, ginger, cloves, and salt.
2. Add softened butter (not melted) and mix until blended.
3. Gradually add molasses and milk while mixing on low speed for approximately 30 seconds or until combined.
4. Divide dough in half and form balls. Wrap each with plastic wrap and refrigerate for two hours or overnight. For faster results, freeze for about 20 minutes until firm.
5. Preheat oven to 350°F (176°C). Line two baking sheets with parchment paper.
6. Remove a dough ball from fridge/freezer. Roll out dough. Lightly flour with rolling pin to 1/2-inch thickness. Cut gingerbread with your favorite cookie cutter and place 2 inches apart on prepared baking sheets.
7. Refrigerate for ten minutes.
8. Bake cookies for 10-12 minutes depending on your oven. Avoid overbaking!
9. Transfer cookies to a wire rack, allowing them to cool to room temperature before frosting

PLEASE NOTE: THIS RECIPE SHOULD ONLY BE PREPARED WITH ADULT SUPERVISION.

MR. GRAHAM'S GINGERBREAD FROSTING:

2 large egg whites at room temperature

3 cups powdered sugar sifted

½ teaspoon cream of tartar

INSTRUCTIONS:

1. In a mixing bowl, whip egg whites until foamy. Then add cream of tartar. Continue to mix for 30 seconds.
2. Add powdered sugar a little bit at a time mixing well.
3. Once the powdered sugar is incorporated, turn mixer to high and continue beating until thick and the icing holds its shape (about 3-5 minutes).
4. Store in a glass bowl. Cover tightly with saranwrap. For best results, use a disposable frosting bag for decorative touches.

PLEASE NOTE: THIS RECIPE SHOULD ONLY BE PREPARED WITH ADULT SUPERVISION.

Mr. Graham's Hot Cocoa With Marshmallows

PREP: 5 MINUTES

SERVING: 4-5

INGREDIENTS:

3 Tablespoons Unsweetened Cocoa Powder

¼ Cup Sugar

4 Cups Whole Milk – Substitute With Almond or Coconut Milk If Desired

¼ Teaspoon Vanilla

Miniature Marshmallows

A Dash of Cinnnamon if Desired

1. Gather the ingredients.
2. In a medium saucepan, heat milk to scalding.
3. While milk is heating, blend cocoa and sugar in a small bowl.
4. Mix about 1/3 cup hot milk into cocoa and sugar mixture.
5. Pour cocoa mixture into hot milk in a saucepan. Add vanilla and whisk until blended.
6. Serve cocoa topped with mini marshmallows a dash cinnamon and sift a dash of cocoa powder over marshmallows, if desired.

PLEASE NOTE: THIS RECIPE SHOULD ONLY BE PREPARED WITH ADULT SUPERVISION.

ACKNOWLEDGMENTS
To my husband Mike, thank you for supporting my dream of storytelling.
To our two sons, Mike and Dan, who have blossomed into my insightful teachers.
To my sister-in-law, Cami Murace, for her skillful editing and her unwavering support since the very beginning.
To my friend and editor, Jim Meany, esteemed Professor of Grammar.
To my late Uncle Joe Agostino, who always believed in me.

ABOUT THE AUTHOR
Pina Basone, also known as Pina Bird, grew up in Connecticut and developed a passion for storytelling at an early age. Throughout her career, Pina has continually reinvented herself while instilling in her children the belief that hard work and self-confidence can make any dream come true. Her stories are inspired by her own experiences and fond memories of childhood. This is Pina's fourth children's book, following titles like Fred the Super Friend, Fred the Super Saves the Mangroves, and Chicken Livers and Artichokes. Her books are available at www.pinabirdbooks.com, Amazon and local bookstores. She hopes that you will enjoy each book's heartwarming messages and valuable lessons.

ABOUT THE ILLUSTRATOR
Jennifer Kirkham, a British freelance illustrator, is a graduate of the prestigious Glasgow School of Art. She works from her home studio in the Northeast of England, concentrating primarily on book illustrations and animation design. She attributes her enduring passion for drawing to the influence of her late grandfather, Ken Kirkham, a gifted artist.

www.ingramcontent.com/pod-product-compliance
Lightning Source LLC
Chambersburg PA
CBHW041705160426
43209CB00017B/1751